Why Is This Day Special?
A Birthday

Jillian Powell

Smart Apple Media

First published in 2005 by Franklin Watts
96 Leonard Street, London EC2A 4XD

Franklin Watts Australia
45–51 Huntley Street, Alexandria, NSW 2015

Series editor: Sarah Peutrill, Art director: Jonathan Hair, Designer: Ian Thompson, Picture researcher: Diana Morris, Reading consultant: Margaret Perkins, Institute of Education, University of Reading

Picture credits: Art Directors/Trip: 18b. Jon Burbank/Hutchison: 27b. Jon Burbank/Image Works/Topham: 24b. Fritz Curzon/PAL/Topham: 26. John Dakers/Eye Ubiquitous: 20tr. Gretel Ensignia/NAPA/Topham: 7. Sarah Errington/Hutchison: 13bl. Alain Evrard/Alamy: 8. Peter Frischmitt/Argus/Still Pictures: 15. Fiona Good/Art Directors/Trip: 22. Julian Hamilton/NAPA/Topham: 11b. Image Works/Topham: 27t. Gerard Kingma Travel & Nature Photography: 11t. A. Kuznetsov/Art Directors/Trip: 14bl. H. Luther/Art Directors/Trip: 9b. Rob van Nostrand/Perfectphoto: 14tr. Picturepoint/Topham: 12t. Terry Prekas Photography: 25. Oleg Prikhodko Photography: 19b. Francisco Rangel/Image Works/Topham: 16b. Helene Rogers/Art Directors/Trip: 24t. Jorgen Schytte/Scanpix: 20bl. Topham: 10. Peter Treanor/Art Directors/Trip: 13tr. Michael S. Yamashita/Corbis: 9t.

Published in the United States by Smart Apple Media
2140 Howard Drive West, North Mankato, Minnesota 56003

Library of Congress Cataloging-in-Publication Data

Powell, Jillian.
A birthday / by Jillian Powell.
p. cm. — (Why is this day special?)
Includes index.
ISBN-13 : 978-1-58340-947-3
1. Birthdays—Juvenile literature. I. Title.

GT2340.P68 2006
394.2—dc22   2005051622

9 8 7 6 5 4 3 2 1

Contents

Everyone's special day

Birthdays are the anniversaries of the days people were born. Around the world, people celebrate their birthdays in many different ways.

Children enjoying a birthday party.

For some people, birthdays are just about having fun with their friends and family. To celebrate, they may be given gifts and have a party.

> **❝** *My dad blew up lots of balloons for my birthday party. I think it was hard work!* **❞**
>
> *Jessica, age 8*

In some countries, there are traditional customs for wishing people happiness and a long life on their birthday.

When people belong to a religion, they may also have special ways to celebrate.

The birthday of an important person can be a time for many people to celebrate.

Children may wear a button on their birthday to show their age.

In Britain, soldiers parade in London to celebrate the Queen's birthday.

First birthday

For some people, a first birthday is very special.

In Korea, this is the only true birthday that children celebrate. After that, they celebrate being a year older at New Year in January or February.

On their first birthday, Koreans are given presents such as cotton for long life, money for wealth, and a notebook for learning. Family and friends have a party to wish them a long and happy life.

A Korean boy celebrates his first birthday.

" When I was one, my mom and dad put my handprints on a birthday tablecloth. Now we do the same every year to see how much bigger I am! "

Grace, age 8

In China and Vietnam, all babies celebrate their first birthday at the first New Year after they are born. They count their age from each New Year that follows.

A Chinese family celebrates its baby's first birthday.

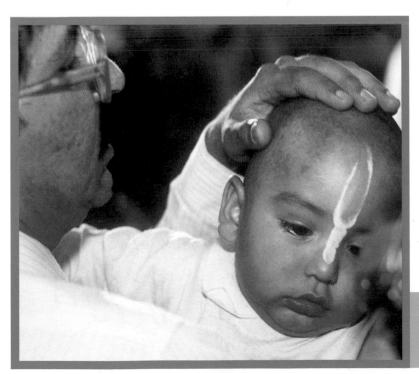

Some Hindu families shave their baby son's head when he is one year old. This is because Hindus believe that people live many lives, and that cutting off the baby's hair takes away any badness from past lives.

This little boy has had his head shaved.

Special birthdays

Around the world, people celebrate different special birthdays.

In Japan, there is a festival for children when they are age three, five, and seven. The children are given candy in bags decorated with cranes and turtles, which are animals that have long lives.

> *" My parents gave me candy in a bag on my seventh birthday. The candy lasted a long time! "*
>
> *Keiko, age 8*

These Japanese girls are dressed for the 3,5,7 festival.

In Holland, children celebrate a "crown birthday" when they are five, and every five years after. They receive a big present, and their chair is decorated with flowers and balloons.

A Dutch boy wears a paper crown to show that it is his special birthday.

In Britain, when people reach their 100th birthday, they receive congratulations from the Queen!

These twin sisters reached their 100th birthday.

Coming of age

Many people have special celebrations as children grow into adults, or come of age.

When they are 13, Jewish boys celebrate their bar mitzvah. They go to the synagogue to read and pray and then have a party with their family to celebrate becoming an adult. Jewish girls may celebrate their bat mitzvah when they are 12.

A Jewish boy reads from the holy book the Torah at his bar mitzvah.

" *I went to my brother's bar mitzvah. It was a really special day, and I can't wait for mine!* "
Oliver, age 11

In some countries, people celebrate their coming of age at the age of 18 or 21.

Some people receive keys for their 21st birthday. This is a symbol to show they are now able to open the door to adult life.

Some girls have a special birthday when they are 15. In Cuba, they have a big party. They wear a pink dress and their first high-heeled shoes, and they dance the waltz with their father.

This girl in Cuba is on the way to her 15th birthday party.

Ceremonies are held for groups of children when they become 13 or older in parts of Africa. They learn the customs, laws, songs, and dances of their tribe. Sometimes they take tests to show how much they have learned or how strong they have become.

These Makonde girls are dressed for their coming of age ceremony in Tanzania.

Birthday wishes

There are many different ways to wish people good luck on their birthday.

In Canada, they have butter rubbed on their nose, because this will make them too slippery for bad luck to catch them!

> " I open my cards, then I get to have the butter surprise! "
>
> Hayley, age 9

This Canadian girl is having butter rubbed onto her nose for her 12th birthday.

In Nepal, people have a spot of colored rice yogurt put on their forehead for good luck.

A child in Nepal on her birthday.

Children may be given the "birthday bumps." Their friends hold their arms and legs and throw them up and down. They are thrown once for every year of their age, and one more time for luck.

In Israel, small children are lifted up and down in a chair.

Family and friends give birthday bumps using a big sheet.

Birthday parties

Many people celebrate their birthday by having a party.

At children's parties, there are often balloons, party favors, and hats.

Everyone dresses in his or her party clothes and brings birthday presents and cards. In Mexico and Cuba, there is often a piñata. This is a toy in the shape of an animal or a star that is filled with candy.

Piñatas are often animal-shaped. The birthday child wears a blindfold and has to hit the piñata with a stick until it breaks open and the candy falls out.

In many countries, everyone sings a happy birthday song to the birthday girl or boy.

Then they play games such as "Pin the Tail on the Donkey" or "Musical Chairs." There is often dancing to music, too.

> *For my birthday party, we had a sleepover. I stayed awake for a long time because I was so excited.*
>
> Naomi, age 9

"Blind Man's Bluff" is a popular party game in Britain.

Birthday foods

Birthdays are often celebrated with special foods and meals.

At children's parties, there may be lots of treats such as cookies, ice cream, and cake.

Party foods are often sweet and colorful.

Children in China eat noodles for lunch on their birthday. Friends and relatives are often invited to share the noodles. They are thought to be a lucky food that brings long life.

This Chinese boy is having noodles for his birthday.

A cake is the most important food in many birthday celebrations. The birthday person makes a wish and tries to blow out all the candles together. In many countries, the birthday person cuts or eats the first slice of cake. In Brazil, they give the first slice to their best friend or someone in their family.

A birthday cake often has frosting and candles. There is one candle for each year of the person's age and sometimes one more for luck.

In Russia, people eat birthday pies that have a birthday greeting written on the crust.

This Russian birthday pie has a child's name on top.

Birthday customs

There are many different birthday customs around the world.

In Japan, a child is dressed in new clothes for his or her birthday.

> This little girl in Japan is wearing a new kimono for her birthday.

In Denmark, families put out flags to show that someone at home is having a birthday.

A Danish family has flags at the table for a birthday meal.

All over the world, families and friends give cards and presents to congratulate people on their birthday.

A pile of birthday presents waits to be unwrapped.

When I have a birthday, I wake and find a ribbon tied to my bed. I have to follow the ribbon, and it takes me to my presents!

Natalie, age 10

Some babies are given a charm bracelet on their first birthday. They are given a new charm each year for their bracelet as a special keepsake.

A charm bracelet can have new charms added on each birthday.

Birth signs and birthstones

Birthdays give us a horoscope, a Chinese animal sign, and a birthstone.

Astrologers study the time and date of a person's birth. They look at the position of the stars and the planets to figure out the person's horoscope. They believe this will show what will happen to them in the future.

When a Hindu baby is born, a priest or astrologer writes his or her horoscope. This helps the parents choose the baby's name.

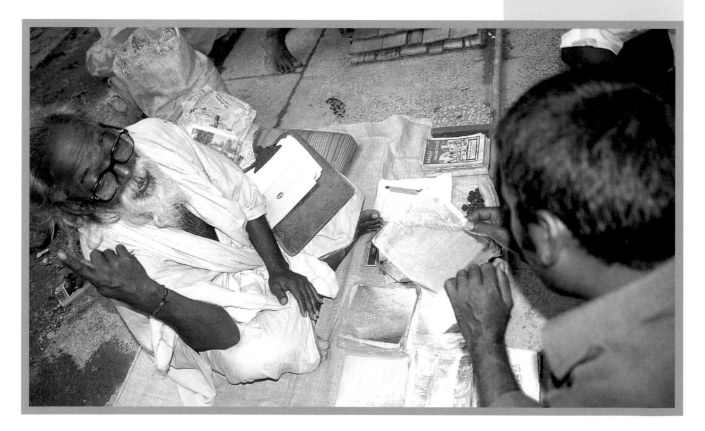

Dates of birth also give people a star sign, which some people believe shows what a person will be like. There are 12 star signs.

The year people are born gives them a Chinese animal sign. There are 12 animal signs, and each one comes around every 12 years. The Chinese believe that animal signs affect the way people behave.

The 12 animal signs in the Chinese calendar, from top to bottom, are: Rat, Ox, Tiger, Rabbit, Dragon, Snake, Horse, Ram, Monkey, Cock, Dog, and Pig.

“ *I was born in the Year of the Ram. That means I'm caring!* ”

Lee, age 11

The month people are born also decides the birthstone. Some people believe that wearing a birthstone such as a ruby is lucky.

Many people like to wear their birthstone in jewelry.

Birthdays and religion

People belonging to certain religions do not celebrate birthdays. For others, birthdays are a time for prayer and giving thanks.

On their birthday, Hindu children take flowers to a temple. The priest gives the child a blessing.

This child is carrying a rose to a temple in Calcutta, India.

In Japan, Shinto children visit a shrine on their third, fifth, and seventh birthday.

A Shinto priest blesses a child at the 3,5,7 festival.

Many people in Greece are named after a saint. They celebrate their Name Day instead of their birthday. This is the day when people celebrate the life of the saint they are named after. Family and friends visit and bring gifts.

> **"** *My name is Barbara, so I celebrate Saint Barbara's day. I have a picture of her on my bedroom wall, and I put flowers under it and light a candle on my Name Day.* **"**
> Barbara, age 9

A family in Greece celebrates Name Day with a special meal.

Muslims, Rastafarians, and Jehovah's Witnesses do not celebrate birthdays. They believe it is right to celebrate important religious festivals rather than the special days of individuals.

Important birthdays

Many important religious festivals celebrate birthdays.

Christmas celebrates the birth of Jesus Christ. Christians go to church to sing songs called "carols" and give thanks for the birth of Jesus. At schools, children put on Nativity plays to tell the story of Jesus's birth.

" When we had a Nativity play at my school last Christmas, I was Joseph. "

Jordan, age 8

Children taking part in a Nativity play.

At Janmashtami in August or September, Hindus celebrate the birth of Lord Krishna. They decorate their homes and temples with pictures of his life. They pray, sing hymns, and celebrate with a feast.

Men climb to reach pots of butter hung from buildings in Mumbai, India. This reminds people of a story about Krishna when he was a boy.

Buddhists celebrate the birth of Buddha on Wesak, or Buddha Day, which falls in April, May, or June. On this day, Buddhists clean and decorate their homes and light lanterns or candles. They pray and learn about the Buddha's life and teaching.

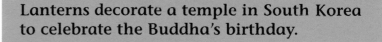

Lanterns decorate a temple in South Korea to celebrate the Buddha's birthday.

Glossary

anniversary the date on which something happened in a past year.

astrologers people who study the stars and planets to predict the future.

bar mitzvah a ceremony that marks a Jewish boy becoming a man.

bat mitzvah a ceremony that marks a Jewish girl becoming a woman.

carol a song sung to celebrate Jesus's birth.

ceremonies celebrations of important events.

Chinese New Year a festival held in January or February in China that marks a new year based on the Chinese lunar (moon months) calendar.

custom an act that is repeated over many years.

horoscope what may happen in people's lives based on the position of the stars and planets when they were born.

Jehovah's Witnesses a member of a particular branch of Christianity.

keepsake a gift that is kept for a long time.

Nativity a play telling the story of the birth of Jesus.

prayer words said when a person talks to God.

priest someone who leads religious worship.

saint a holy person in the Christian religion. People are not called saints until after they have died.

synagogues a building where Jewish people go to pray and study.

waltz a kind of dance.

Religions in this book

Buddhism
Follower: Buddhist
Important figure: Siddhartha Gautama, the Buddha
Gods: None
Places of worship: Viharas (temples or monasteries), stupas (shrines)
Holy books: Tirpitaka (Pali Canon), Diamond Sutra, and others

Christianity
Follower: Christian
Important figure: Jesus Christ
God: One God as Father, Son, and Holy Spirit
Places of worship: Churches, cathedrals, and chapels
Holy book: The Bible

Hinduism
Follower: Hindu
Gods and goddesses: Many, including Brahma (the Creator), Vishnu (the Protector), and Shiva (the Destroyer)
Places of worship: Mandirs (temples) and shrines
Holy books: Vedas, Upanishads, Ramayana, Mahabharata

Islam
Follower: Muslim
Important figure: The Prophet Muhammad
God: Allah
Place of worship: Mosque
Holy book: The Koran

Judaism
Follower: Jew
Important figures: Abraham, Isaac, Jacob, and Moses
God: One God, the creator
Place of worship: Synagogues
Holy books: Tenakh, Torah, Talmud

Sikhism
Follower: Sikh
Important figure: Guru Nanak
God: One God
Place of worship: Gurdwaras
Holy book: Guru Granth Sahib

Shinto
Follower: Shintoist
Important figures: Kami—spirits of nature, gods, ancestors, and dead heroes
Places of worship: Temples in Japan

Rastafarianism
Follower: Rastafarian
Important figures: Marcus Garvey, Haile Selassie
God: Jah, living god for the black race
Places of worship: None
Holy book: The Bible

Index